WINDOW COVERING BASICS

*How To Achieve Custom Looks
With Ready-made Products*

by

Carolyn Lee DeFever

Paisley Publishing,
San Antonio, Texas

WINDOW COVERING BASICS

Printed and bound in the
United States of America.
Line drawings Fig. 1 - 30, 32- 35, 37, 39, 43, 44,
47 - 51, 62 - 65, 72- 75, and Pages 93,94
Courtesy of Kirsch
Continental Curtain Rod® Reg. TM Cooper Industries, Inc.

Photographs Courtesy of Croscill Home Fashions

Book Design and Illustrations
Fig. 31, 36, 38, 40 - 42, 45, 46, 52 - 61, and 66 - 71, by
Jason Roberts & Associates
San Antonio, Texas.

Published by Paisley Publishing
1802 Paisley,
San Antonio, Texas, 78231

Third Edition.

Library of Congress Catalog Card Number: 91-90553
ISBN Number 0-9626117-3-5

Table of Contents

INTRODUCTION

The prospect of doing your own windows can be overwhelming. But, being your own decorator isn't as difficult as you may think. You can do it with the help of this guide. You will be able to properly measure your windows, buy the appropriate size draperies or curtains, the right amount of panels or valances or tiers, and the correct hardware. You will also be able to install your selected window treatment to achieve a custom look. The formulas are simple and logical.

You may wish to use "Window Covering Basics" as a reference manual and simply turn to the section relevant to the project you have at hand. However, many suggested treatments in the sections on options may be applicable to more than one type of window covering. Throughout this guide you will find valuable "Reader's Tips". The simplified illustrations will remove the mystery from those seemingly complicated treatments such as bay windows, corner windows, and French doors, and stimulate your imagination, as well.

Although this guide offers a multitude of decorating tips and options, the primary value is in what comes "after the idea". The most expensive window treatments completely lose their value when improperly installed. Using the wrong drapery hooks, for example, could destroy the overall effect of your window treatment. You will find the section on "Common Mistakes" invaluable, and undoubtedly find yourself correcting some of these problems on existing window treatments in your home.

You will be able to achieve custom looking window treatments for a fraction of the cost of custom services. The only talent involved is knowing what to buy and how to install it. You don't have to know how to sew on a button. **There is absolutely no expertise required that is not between the covers of "WINDOW COVERING BASICS."**

Preface

Windows play a large part in the overall decorating scheme of a home, creating illusions of spaciousness with light colored treatments that blend and duplicate wall coloring, or vividly dramatic focal points with bright colors and prints. Attractive window treatments add real value to your home and makes it more marketable.

Ambiance is greatly controlled by window coverings, as well. The psychological effect of textures and colors can be surprising. Imagine the striking change in ambiance from a modern decor with bright white walls and white mini blinds to, for example, antique white walls and dark velvet draperies with ornate top treatments.

Just for fun, think about how a room makes you feel when you first walk into it. Try it at a friend's house. Think about what you want to accomplish; the feel and ambiance you want to project. Decide what fits in best with your life style and with what decor you would feel most comfortable. Window covering treatments are a long term investment. Choose colors that you really like, possibly even colors that compliment you personally.

Unless you're going to be hiring custom decorators, or you're a competent seamstress, most decorating books will be of little value. If you have decided to decorate with ready-made products, your best course of action will be to start looking in ready-made drapery departments. The selections today are outstanding.

There Are Basically Three Ways To Go About Decorating Windows:

1. Custom:
A decorator will come to your home and show samples, offer opinions and options; measure and install.

2. Made-to-Measure:
You measure and take your measurements to a department store; choose your fabrics or other window coverings from their selection and they order to your specifications. You install. A word of caution about made-to-measure: a good amount of expertise is required on the part of the sales associate. Try to qualify the person you are working with. Made-to-measure is not returnable.

3. Ready-Made:
Draperies or products that are pre-made and available in specific widths and lengths; may be returned or exchanged.

This guide deals primarily with ready-made window treatments. Ready-mades are the least expensive and in most cases can be taken home when purchased. The only exception is when a ready-made size has to be special ordered; even then, it is still a ready-made product and may be returned if it proves unsatisfactory, if you change your mind about color, or if you mistakenly ordered the wrong size.

WINDOW COVERING TERMINOLOGY

1. *Return*—
That part of fabric which covers the area from the end of a curtain rod back to the wall.

2. *Clearance*—
Rod clearance is the distance from the wall to the back of the rod; not to be confused with returns. **See Fig. 1**

Fig. 1

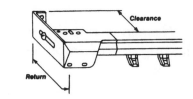

3. *Overlap*—
That part of fabric which rides the master carrier of a traverse rod and overlaps in the center when closed.

Fig. 2

4. *Rod-Pocket*—
Generally refers to pocket depths of 2-1/2 inches or less and is designed to use a standard curtain rod.

Fig. 3

5. *Pole-Top*—
Generally refers to pocket depths of 3 or 3-1/2 inches and is designed to be used with a 2-1/2 inch deep curtain rod or 1-3/8 inch diameter pole.

6. Continental®—

The term continental has come to be synonymous with the wide rod-pocket curtains or valances. Continental®I and Continental® II are registered trade names for Kirsch curtain rods 4-1/2 and 2-1/2 inches in depth, respectively.

Fig 4—Continental®II   Fig. 5—Continental®I

7. Header, or Heading—

The top part of draperies that accommodates the pleating.

Fig. 6.
Pinch-Pleated Header.

In curtains other than pinch-pleated,
the header is that top portion of fabric above the rod-pocket.

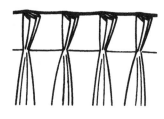

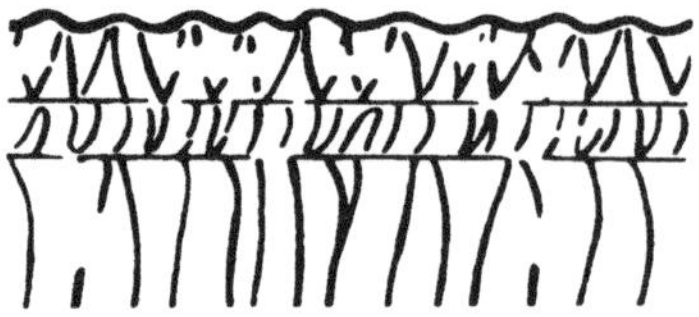

Fig. 7.
Rod-Pocket Header

8. Buckram Header—

Buckram is a coarse stiff cloth used in pinch-pleated drapery headings.

9. Undertreatment—

In layered window treatments,
usually the covering nearer the glass.

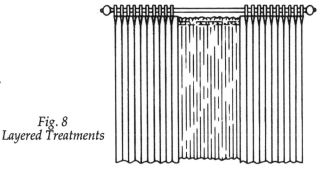

Fig. 8
Layered Treatments

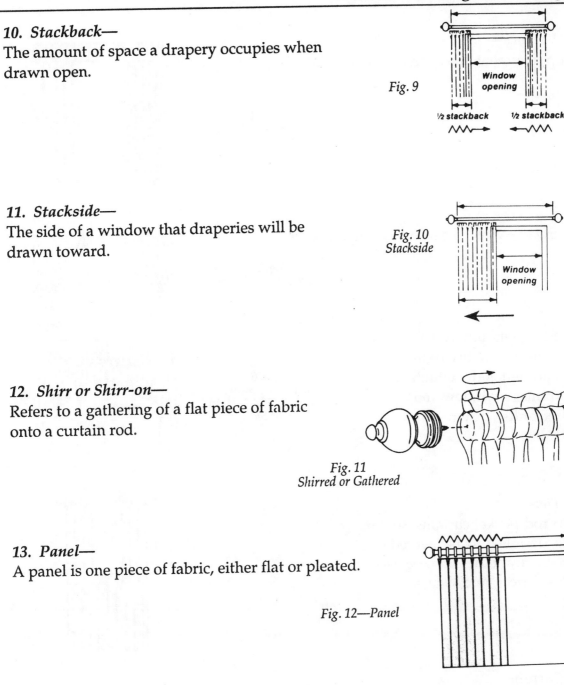

10. Stackback—
The amount of space a drapery occupies when drawn open.

Fig. 9

Window opening

½ stackback   ½ stackback

11. Stackside—
The side of a window that draperies will be drawn toward.

Fig. 10
Stackside

Window opening

12. Shirr or Shirr-on—
Refers to a gathering of a flat piece of fabric onto a curtain rod.

Fig. 11
Shirred or Gathered

13. Panel—
A panel is one piece of fabric, either flat or pleated.

Fig. 12—Panel

14. Pair—
A pair is two panels of equal width and length.

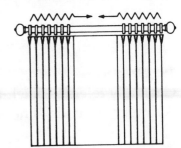

Fig. 13—Pair

15. Valance—
A top treatment that frames a window.

Fig. 14
Valance Frames Window

16. Swag—verb: To draw over to one side.

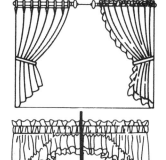

Fig. 15
Swags To Each Side

Swag—noun: A top treatment with a right and left side which frames a window and extends down the sides.

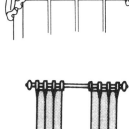

Fig. 16
One Pair Of Swags, Consisting Of A Left And Right Side.

17. Tier—
Short rod-pocket curtains, sold in pairs, designed to be layered one row above another or to be used with valances and swags.

Fig. 17—Tiers

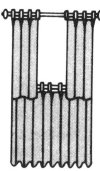

18. Curtain—
Refers to rod-pocket-top styles designed to be shirred onto a curtain rod.

19. Drapery—
Generally refers to pinch-pleated-top window coverings, but not exclusively. A drapery is made of heavier fabrics than curtains and is often lined.

COMMON MISTAKES

1. Measuring the bottom of a pinch-pleated drapery to determine replacement size:
Draperies should always be measured at the pleated top. A pinch-pleated drapery must fit the traverse rod exactly.

2. Counting pleats in draperies to determine replacement size:
Standard pleating in ready-made draperies is generally four inches apart, but sometimes five. In custom draperies pleats could be as little as two or three inches apart.

3. Hanging short draperies too short:
The view from the outside should always be considered. The hem in ready-made draperies is generally around five inches and should always hang below the window.

4. Installing curtain rod too low:
Keeping the outside view in mind, any type of curtain or drapery should be hung a minimum of four inches above the window. This will prevent hooks and header from being visible from the outside.

5. Installing curtain rods too close to side of window: This creates a number of undesirable effects: lack of light control and privacy, unsightly effect from outside view (edges of drapery may be visible); no stackback.

6. Installing undertreatment rods too high or too low:
Sheer curtains should not be more than one inch shorter than draperies; one half inch is ideal. A separate curtain rod can be installed under a traverse rod, however, there is a utility rod designed specifically to be attached to a traverse rod for this purpose and, in using this, your undersheer will automatically be at the proper length. A combination rod is even easier. It is a traverse rod with a stationary rod attached for shirr-on curtains.

7. Not allowing additional return for combination, double traverse, or valance rods:
The amount of return calculated for drapery installation depends on the type of rod used. In general calculations, a total of 12 inches is added to the measurement of the rod from end to end. Four inches is allowed for overlap and four inches for each return.

These calculations are figured assuming a standard traverse rod is used. A combination rod extends to five inches from the wall and a double traverse rod to six inches. A valance rod can extend to 8-1/4 inches. The additional inches must be added to your returns.

8. *Neglecting to subtract returns from pinch-pleated undersheers:*
Sometimes pinch-pleated sheers are used as a primary treatment, in which case returns and overlap are considered in the overall measurement. However, when pinch-pleated sheers are used as an undertreatment on a double traverse rod, returns are not used, but overlap is.

9. *Not using returns on decorator rods:*
Whether using decorative traverse rods or cafe rods with rings, a return is required. On cafe rods, a cuphook or screweye may be affixed to the wall.

10. *Not using rods with correct clearance from wall:*
Draperies are often layered; each layer must clear the other to assure proper function. Available clearance ranges from a sash rod which lays directly on the wall, to a valance rod which extends to about 8-1/4 inches from the wall.

11. *Extending rods too close to maximum width:*
The weight of draperies should be considered in determining how far it is safe to extend your curtain rod. The use of center supports will affect this determination, as well.

12. *Buying draperies too small or too large:*
Pinch-pleated draperies must fit the traverse rod exactly. 12 inches must be added to the rod measurement, (face of the rod, from end to end) to accommodate returns and overlap. Drapery fullness is determined by the amount of widths of fabric used. The more widths of fabric used, the closer together the pleats are. A drapery will not look fuller by using a larger size.

13. *Neglecting to consider stackback:*
Stackback is the portion of drapery that hangs or stacks against the wall when draperies are opened. When stackback is not considered into the overall drapery width, one third of the window will be covered when the draperies are drawn open.

14. *Centering rod over patio doors for one-way-draws:*
A one-way-draw rod should be placed four inches beyond the door on the side that opens, and the remainder on the stackside. Stackback on one-way-draws always goes to one side only.

15. *Using wrong drapery hooks or incorrect placement:*
Drapery hooks are designed for conventional or decorator rods and closed or open drapery headers. A closed header is completely enclosed in the drapery lining and requires a sharp pointed hook that will pierce the fabric. A short pointed hook is used for decorator rods and a longer one for conventional traverse rods. The longer hook holds the header upright. An open header requires a hook that slides around the pleat like a bobby pin. These hooks are designed specifically for a conventional or decorator rod. The top of draperies hang below a decorator rod and conceal a conventional rod. A small pointed pin-on hook can be used with any drapery, providing the placement is correct. Hook placement guides are usually available in drapery departments.

16. *Using wrong rods for which rod-pocket was designed:*
Shirr-on curtains use rods varying from 3/8 inches to 4-1/2 inches in width or diameter. A great many ready-made curtains now come with a three inch rod-pocket, designed to be used with either the 2-1/2 inch wide curtain rod or decorative poles. This information is not always specified on the package.

17. *Under-dressing windows with gathered panels or tiers:*
This creates a skimpy look. The hallmark of a custom look is abundance—fullness. The rule is, "two to four times window width," depending on thickness of fabric being used and degree of privacy wanted, or effect desired.

18. *Neglecting to use hard window treatments on high sun impact windows:*
Hard window treatments would be mini blinds, verticals, pleated shades, woven woods, roller shades, wood blinds or shutters. The sun is extremely damaging to fabric. The use of hard window coverings can lengthen the life of draperies or curtains for years.

PINCH-PLEATED DRAPERIES

How to Measure

Ready-made window coverings are measured width by length. The width measurement always comes first. A drapery 100x84 is 100 inches wide and 84 inches long.

Reader Tip
Always use a metal tape measure. Cloth or plastic tapes will stretch and result in inaccurate measurements.

There are several ways to go about measuring for ready-made draperies. If replacing existing draperies, you may wish to measure the width of your old draperies at the pleated top. Counting the pleats is generally not accurate because the spacing between pleats can vary from two to five inches. However, four to five inches is common in ready-made draperies. Pleated draperies should fit the rod exactly. There is no way to add extra fullness to a pleated drapery short of decreasing the distance between pleats. If rods are in place, measure the face of the rod from end to end. Also measure the rod returns—the area where the drapery wraps around the end of the rod to the wall.

The return on a regular traverse rod is generally four inches, a combination rod (traverse with a straight rod for undersheers attached) is five inches, and a double traverse rod is six inches. Be sure to add returns on both ends.

Do not confuse rod clearance with returns.
See Fig. 1 Window Covering Terminology.

The general rule is to take the rod measurement (end to end) and add 12 inches. The twelve inches includes the returns on each side and the overlap in the center. 4+4+4=12.

For length, measure from top of rod to floor, or with a decorative traverse rod, measure from the bottom of the hook slide to floor. In either case, the measurement should be 84 inches to accommodate ready-made draperies—or 95 inches from the ceiling to the floor.

When starting with bare window measurements, (no rods in place or when rods will be replaced) measure the actual window opening. If the window is framed, measure the frame. A minimum of 20 inches is added to this measurement. Also measure from the top of the window to the floor. Be aware of the amount of wall space available on either side of the window for stackback, if desired.

One third of your drapery width, minus 12, 14, or 16 inches, depending on type of rod, divided in half will determine the maximum amount of wall space needed on each side.

Any type rod used for pleated draperies should be placed a minimum of four inches beyond the window on each side and not less than four inches above the top of the window. The easiest way to determine the height of rod placement for floor length draperies is to measure 84-1/2 inches up from the floor. The depth of carpeting differs and this will be a factor in rod placement. The 1/2 inch is for clearance for easy operation. The top of the drapery should be even with the top of a conventional rod. When using a decorative rod, the top of the drapery should cover the ring slides, but not the rings.

Ceiling to floor draperies—

Measure from ceiling to floor and subtract one inch for clearance. The one inch allows 1/2 inch at the ceiling and 1/2 inch at the floor. Only one length is available in ready-made draperies—95 inches, designed to accommodate eight foot ceilings.

When measuring for patio panels you will have a return on only one side and no overlap. Stackback will be on one side only. *See Patio Door Panels.*

Hanging your draperies:

Always start at the master slide, moving toward the wall. Do not skip rings or slides, because you will not want extras interfering with drapery function. Instead, remove them through the end gate. Always use pin-on hooks at master slides and returns.

Breaking the header:

The importance of this function can not be emphasized strongly enough. A stiff buckram lining is used in the heading of pinch-pleated draperies. It must not be allowed to break at random; to do so will prevent the proper function of the traverse rod. The header will be broken either toward the window or away from the window, depending on the type of rod used. A conventional rod will require breaking the header away from the window. A decorative rod will require breaking the header toward the window. To break the header, place your finger or the side of your hand in the center of the flat space between pleats and hand press firmly. Repeat between each pleat except the return and the pleat riding the master carrier.

Miller Curtain Company

What Size to Buy

When working with ready-made draperies it is important to know that you will be making your window fit the draperies rather than finding draperies to fit your windows.

Ready-made draperies are available in specific widths, most commonly in increments of 25, starting at 50 inches. Most common widths are 50, 75, 100, 125, and 150 inches. Some drapery widths are made in increments of 24; that is, 48, 72, 96, 120, and 144 inches.

There is a simple formula. When working with actual window opening measurements, using a standard traverse rod, add a minimum of 20 inches and buy the next available size.

To explain, the 20 inches that is added to the actual window measurement breaks down like this: 12 inches for overlap and returns, plus four inches for rod placement on each side of the window.

Chances are you won't find a ready-made drapery that will be exactly 20 inches larger than your window. Perhaps this is by design because it allows for stackback.

Stackback is the amount of space a drapery occupies when drawn open. Allowing for stackback enables more of the window glass to be exposed, which is especially desirable if there is a pleasant view, if more light is enjoyed, or if you simply want your window to appear larger. Stackback creates a more custom look.

Reader Tip

The average stackback of a drapery is about 1/3 of the drapery width. This will vary depending on pleat spacing and bulk of fabric.

There is no such thing as a standard size window, but for an example let's take a window that measures 60 inches. Add the standard 20 inches and you have 80 inches. Draperies will be available in 75 or 100 inches. You will need to buy the 100 inch drapery. The 20 inches left over will be divided and the rod placement becomes 14 inches beyond the window on each side, instead of four.

Ready-made draperies are available in floor to ceiling lengths, 95 inches; floor length, 84 inches (designed to be placed about four inches above most windows); 72, 63, 54, 45, and sometimes 36 inch lengths.

Options:

Pinch-pleated draperies are sold in pairs or patio panels. A 100 inch pair consists of two, 50 inch panels. A panel, or patio panel, is all in one piece.

Pairs are used with center-draw traverse rods, or in other decorative ways, split in the center. Pinch-pleated draperies can also be used as decorative stationary side panels, hung on a traverse rod or plain curtain rod. The width used is strictly a matter of choice. Side panels are generally used with a valance and undertreatment. One should be careful not to use panels that are too narrow on large windows. It will create a skimpy appearance. Side panels can be swaged back with tie-backs or left hanging straight.

The return, or wraparound, still applies to side panels, to achieve a finished look.

Draperies can be hung on a decorative rod with optional undertreatments. Valances are not used over decorative rods, but are used over conventional rods. There is nothing attractive about a plain unadorned curtain rod and is best concealed under an attractive valance.

Draperies are available in too many fabrics to mention, but for the most part are blends, fabrics that each have a desirable attribute that in combination with others will give the most desirable results.

Common choices today are antique satins, open weaves, and chintz, all of which may be lined or unlined. Foam-backed draperies are also popular. These draperies do not hang as smoothly as lined draperies, but are much improved in recent years.

Unlike most lined draperies, foam-backed draperies are often washable. They are quite durable and considerably less in cost. It is an excellent choice for heavily sun exposed windows and a popular choice for rentals.

Conventional Traverse Rod

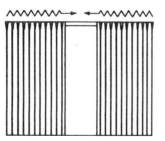

Fig. 18
Two-Way-Draw Pair

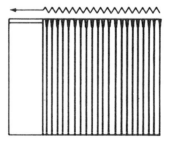

Fig. 19
One-Way-Draw Panel

Decorative Traverse Rods

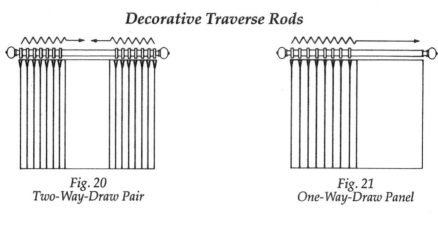

Fig. 20
Two-Way-Draw Pair

Fig. 21
One-Way-Draw Panel

Decorative Cafe Rod

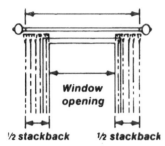

Window opening

½ stackback   ½ stackback

Fig. 22
Stackback
On Each Side

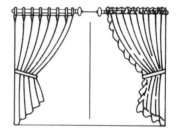

Fig. 23

| Left-Pinch
Pleated Panel
With Rings | Right-Shirr-on
Rod-Pocket Panel
Or Priscilla |

Breaking the Header

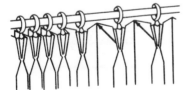

Fig. 24
Decorative Traverse Rod
Breaks Toward the Glass

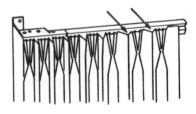

Fig. 25
Conventional Traverse Rod
Breaks Away from the Glass

Reader Tip

Ready-made window coverings are measured width by length.

Patio Door Panels

Patio doors, as referred to throughout this text, are more technically, sliding glass doors; in some parts of the country referred to as Arcadia Doors. Patio doors often cause decorating concerns, but in reality they are wonderful additions to any home, adding value, interest, and decorating opportunities.

Sometimes a patio door doesn't really fit in with the life style of the home owner. In these cases a patio door can be treated as any other window, ignoring the fact that it was intended, by the builder, to be used as a door.

How to Measure

The most common sizes in patio doors are six, seven, and eight foot widths; the glass being in two or three sections. If the rod is in place, measure from end to end and add four inches.

Reader Tip
Unlike a pair of draperies, a patio panel is hung on a one-way-draw rod. There is a return on only one side and no overlap.

If the rod is already in place, it will appear to be lopsided because it will extend far more to one side than the other.

If starting with bare window measurements, first determine which way the panel will stack. If the door opens from the left and slides to the right, the drapery will stack right. If the door opens from the right and slides left, the drapery will stack left. One-way-draw rods will have the draw cord on the side that the drapery stacks: Stack left—cord left. Stack right—cord right.

Once the stack direction is determined, the measurement can be calculated. The importance of the stack direction is to determine the amount of wall space available for stackback.

The rod should be placed four inches away from the door on the opening side and a minimum of four inches on the stackside. To allow more of the glass door to be exposed when the panel is drawn open, stackback must be considered. Stackback is about one third of the drapery width.

What Size to Buy

The three considerations are window size, stackback area available and available ready-made sizes.

The most commonly available size in ready-made patio panels is 100x84. Also available in a smaller selection is the 75x84 and 125x84 sizes.

A six foot door is 72 inches wide. You may think that a 75 inch panel will be sufficient, but not if you want a custom look. With a 75 inch panel, you will have only three inches left over for rod placement and return.

To determine the correct size needed for any patio door, start with the information known: window size plus minimum of four inches on each side for rod placement and one, four inch return. Ready-made sizes available: 75, 100, 125 inches wide.

For a six foot door you have determined that you will need at least 84 inches, and you know that you will need to go up to the next size available. 100x84. This larger size is desirable because you will have excess drapery left over for stackback. Remember that stackback is about 1/3 of drapery width. But now that drapery size has been determined, it also becomes apparent that rod placement will be changed on the stackside. You will only be able to use a ready-made size if there is enough wall space for stackback. It has been determined that a minimum of 84 inches is needed, and that you will be using a 100 inch panel. 100-84=16. Add 16 inches to your original four inches allowed for rod placement on stackside. Your rod will be placed 20 inches away from the door on the stackside. This may not give you complete clearing of the glass when the panel is drawn open, but the effect will be so much more desirable than if your drapery covered a complete third of the glass. The variable in stackback is affected by pleat spacing and drapery thickness.

The length of patio panels is always 84 inches, designed for eight foot ceilings.

Some patio doors have three sections of glass with the center panel opening. In this case you would use a pair of draperies as with any regular window and allow for overlap, returns, and stackback on each side.

Reader Tip

Rods should always be placed a minimum of four inches above window or door glass.

Options:

Most draperies are also available in patio panels. Another recent option is patio priscillas. A patio priscilla is a one piece curtain with a ruffle on each side, designed to shirr-on a rod. Measurements are flat measurements. 150 inches is common for patio priscillas. The priscilla is shirred on a rod to about half the width of the door and swagged back in the direction of the stackside with a tie—often a bow. The valance is then shirred onto the remainder of the same rod, going completely across the door to the end of the rod on the opening side. This treatment is stationary and is not meant to be moved. Half of your door will be exposed at all times.

Conventional Rod

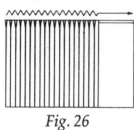

Fig. 26
Coventional Rod
Stacks Left

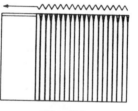

Fig. 27
Coventional Rod
Stacks Right

Decorative Rod

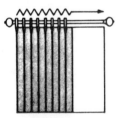

Fig. 28
Decorative Rod
Stacks Left

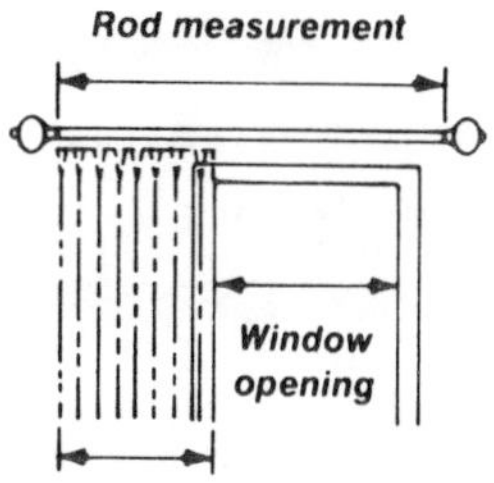

Fig. 30
Stackside

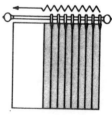

Fig. 29
Decorative Rod
Stacks Right

Fig. 31
Patio Priscilla

A hard window covering, such as a vertical blind, is popular under this kind of treatment. It satisfies the privacy problem and can be very attractive if coordinated well.

UNDERTREATMENTS

An undertreatment is generally the layer closest to the glass. However, with the increasing popularity of hard window treatments, such as mini blinds and shades, the term undertreatment often means more than one thing. For example, a hard window treatment may be covered with a sheer curtain and a lined drapery. The luxury of draperies and sheers need not be sacrificed for the additional benefits of energy conservation or sun and light control of hard window treatments. You can virtually have it all.

Curtains used for undertreatments will be available in rod-pocket or pinch-pleated panels.

Pinch-pleated sheers: Pinch-pleated sheers may be used as a primary drapery. When doing so, the formula for measuring and buying is the same as for draperies *(See Pinch-Pleated Draperies)*. When pinch-pleated sheers are used as an undertreatment, installed on a double traverse rod, the allowance for returns is eliminated; only the overlap is needed.

The size sheer needed will be the measurement of the rod from end to end plus four inches for overlap.

The purpose of a pinch-pleated undertreatment is for having the option of drawing it open. This is frequently done on center-opening patio doors and French doors. Pinch-pleated sheers are also available in patio panels for one-way-draws.

Popular fabrics for undertreatments range from ultra sheer to opaque, and includes the practical seeded voile and exotic laces. Even an additional independent liner is sometimes hung on the undertreatment traverse rod. This is a good way to completely block out all light at will, by using a blackout liner.

An undersheer should never be more than one inch shorter than the drapery. 1/2 inch is ideal. Pleated sheers are offered in the same lengths as draperies, but the widths are usually in increments of 24. That is: 48, 72, 96, 120, and 144 inches.

Shirr-on Undertreatments:
See Rod-Pocket Panel Curtains.

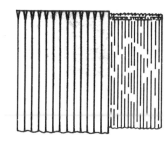

Fig. 32
Rod-Pocket Sheers
Under Pinch-Pleated Draperies

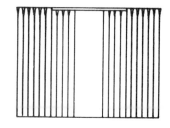

Fig. 33
Pinch-Pleated Sheers Under
Pinch-Pleated Draperies

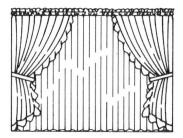

Fig. 34
Rod Pocket Sheers Under
Rod Pocket Priscillas

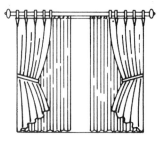

Fig. 35
Pinch-Pleated Sheers
Under Stationary Side Panels

Fig. 36
Balloon Shade Under
Panels and Valance

ROD-POCKET PANEL CURTAINS

A rod-pocket panel is a completely flat piece of fabric with a pocket sewn into the top for the purpose of sliding the curtain rod through. Rod-pocket panels are not designed to be moved. They are strictly stationary panels.

How to Measure:

Measuring for panel curtains is not as critical as for pinch-pleated draperies. Measure your window and add four inches to each side for good coverage. Measure from top of window to floor and add four inches. This is generally a total of 84 inches for eight foot ceilings. Rods should be placed about four inches above window so that headers are not visible from outside. The header of most shirr-on panels, curtains, or tiers, is included in the overall length. However, if the header is two inches or more, it sometimes is not included.

If using short curtains, measure window from top to bottom and add four inches for rod placement above window. Then add an additional five inches so that the hem will completely clear the window. Many hems are five inches and should not be visible from the outside. The inside view would be distracting as well, especially when the sun shines through the window.

What size to buy:

Fullness has not been predetermined by pleating. The degree of fullness is determined by the width of the panel and the number of panels shirred onto the rod.

Two to four times the window width (after adding for rod placement) is the general rule. That may seem broad but there are a number of factors to consider. A lined curtain panel is thicker than a sheer voile panel, so where two times the window width might be perfect for lined chintz, it would take four times the width for sheer fabric, for a full look.

Sheer panels are most often sold singly. If the sheer panel chosen, for example, comes in the most popular size only—60x84— and a 60 inch window is being dressed, two to four panels would be used. Lace and elaborately embroidered panels display their detail more effectively when gathered less tightly. Two to three times the width is adequate.

Rod-pocket panels also come in pairs, but only when designed to be used as a primary curtain, not an undertreatment. The formula is the same—two to four times the window width. Determine the amount of pairs needed based on the window treatment chosen.

Rod-pocket panels may be used as stationary side panels or may go completely across the window and be swaged over to each side with tiebacks.

Stackback may also be considered a factor when using as stationary side panels, allowing the full window to be exposed.

Many rod-pocket sheers have matching valances available and consequently have become very popular as primary window treatments. A hard window covering such as mini blinds or pleated shades is used for privacy.

Use of the correct rod is important. If the rod-pocket is 3 or 3-1/2 inches deep, a 2-1/2 inch wide rod or 1-3/8 inch diameter pole is required. Rod-pockets of 2-1/2 inches or less will use a regular curtain rod.

The wider rod-pockets are sometimes called pole-top instead of rod-pocket-top. When purchasing curtains or panels it would be prudent to check the top to be sure of the type curtain rod required. Using a regular curtain rod in a three inch pocket looks very sloppy, much like an adult's glove on a child's hand.

Fabric Width

Fabric Width

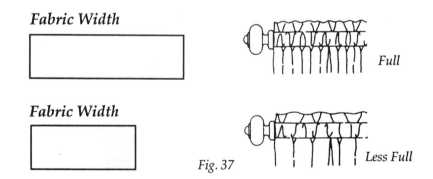

Fig. 37

Full

Less Full

Fig. 38
Two Pair of Pole-Top Draperies over
Rod-Pocket Sheers, Installed on a
Decorative Cafe Rod.

PRISCILLA CURTAINS

Priscillas are, by common definition, ruffled curtains. They are in actuality, panels with one straight side and one ruffled side, with the ruffle extending around the hem. Some priscillas have attached valances. They are sold in pairs and designed to be shirred onto or gathered on a rod, like panels. The straight side goes against the wall and the ruffle is on the glass side. Priscillas are designed specifically to be used with tiebacks, which are always included in the package.

The formula for buying is the same as for rod-pocket panels: two to four times the width to be covered. The rod should be placed at least four inches beyond the window on each side and about four inches above the window.

Priscillas come in the popular floor length, 84 inches long, or below window sill, 63 inches—sometimes available in shorter lengths, 54 and 45 inches.

Priscillas are available in pair widths varying from 96 to 365 inches. Priscillas are now offered in panels; called patio priscillas. One panel, usually about 150 inches wide, is used and it will have a ruffle on both sides. It is used as a stationary panel which goes about half way across the door and is swaged back to one side with a tieback. A short valance is shirred onto the remainder of the same rod to fill up the rest of the space. The valance goes over the side of the door that opens.

Reader Tip

Priscillas may be criss-crossed on a double rod. When doing this, three to four times the window width is mandatory. Each panel must be wide enough to completely cover the window in a gathered fashion.

A valance may also be installed on a separate rod covering the entire window, as a decorating option.

Priscillas often have two length valances available, about 20 inches for floor length curtains and 12 inch lengths for priscillas that only reach the bottom of the window. The shorter valance would also be used on patio doors, so that when the door is in use the valance will not interfere with traffic.

Priscillas generally need to be purchased in pair widths wide enough for the window being treated. They are not meant to be purchased like panels and combined until the desired fullness is achieved. However, any two pairs may be combined by placing the straight side of the panels back-to-back. This method will result in a ruffle on the wall side and the glass side, achieving the same effect as buying two patio priscillas to make a pair.

Tiers are frequently used under priscillas, covering the lower half of the glass or the wall to the floor. Most common lengths are 36 and 45 inches, designed to be used with floor length priscillas. Tiers are sold in pairs and shirr on a rod. Determine the amount of pairs needed to acquire desired fullness, usually the same degree of fullness as the priscilla, or more.

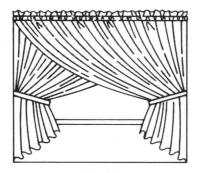

Fig. 39
Use a Double Curtain Rod To
Criss-Cross Panels or Priscillas

Fig. 40
Priscilla with Insert Valance
and Tiers

Fig. 41
Patio Priscilla

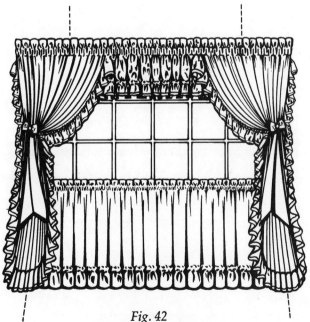

Fig. 42
Two Pair of Priscillas
Placed Back to Back

TIER CURTAINS
CAFE CURTAINS

The term, tier, generally refers to short rod-pocket-top shirr-on curtains. Tiers are sold in pairs to be used on kitchen, bathroom, or other short windows. Tiers come in lengths of 24, 30, 36, and 45 inches. The 45 inch length is usually used under priscillas. Tier curtains can be used as the name implies, and be installed in layers of two or more rows arranged one above another. They are frequently used in conjunction with a valance and or swag.

The definition of some terms change with the kind of window treatment being discussed. Swag is one of those changeable terms. In discussing tiers or kitchen type curtains, a swag is part of the valance that extends down each side of the window, generally about 38 inches long. Swags are sold in pairs with a left and a right side. For larger windows, one or more insert valances are shirred on the rod in between the swag.

Reader Tip

Measuring for tier curtains is the same as for any shirr-on treatment. Two to four times the width of the window is the formula. You would buy as many pairs as is needed to achieve the fullness desired. Keep in mind the thickness of the fabric when determining fullness.

Cafe curtains are tiers with pinch-pleated tops and are often sold with rings attached. These curtains are designed to be used with rings and decorative cafe rods and can easily be moved back and forth by hand. Fullness has been predetermined by pleating but the accuracy of measuring is not as critical as for pinch-pleated draperies. You need only purchase the actual width of the area to be covered, or next size up. Sold in pairs.

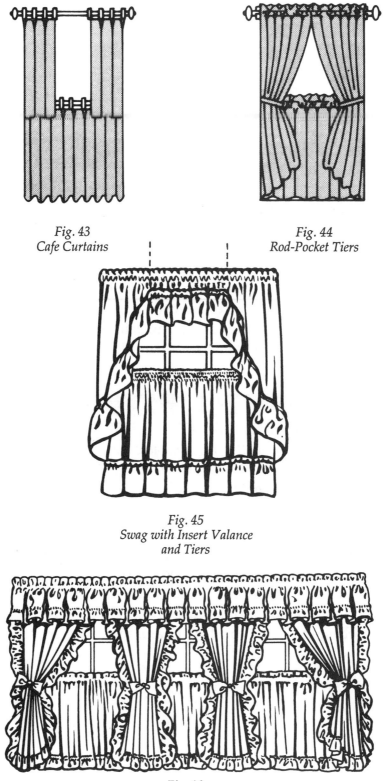

Fig. 43
Cafe Curtains

Fig. 44
Rod-Pocket Tiers

Fig. 45
Swag with Insert Valance
and Tiers

Fig. 46
Multiple Pairs Using 24"Tiers,
45" Tiers and Separate Valances

TOP TREATMENTS

Top treatments are a decorating phenomenon. There was a time when a top treatment translated to a pinch-pleated valance—not anymore. There are so many types of top treatments available it would be impossible to mention them all. The Continental® look is sweeping the country and it is incredibly versatile, making a statement in lined chintz curtains, sheer panels, and priscillas, as well as in valances. The Continental® look is a simple but ingenious concept, utilizing a wider rod pocket; of course requiring a wider curtain rod, and shirring the curtain or valance very tightly over the rod. The effect is wonderful, very much a custom look, because of its ultra fullness.

Continental®I and Continental®II are registered trade names for Kirsch curtain rods. The Continental®I is a curtain rod 4-1/2 inches wide from top to bottom and is designed to be used with a 5 or 5-1/2 inch pocket drapery, curtain, or valance. The Continental®II is a curtain rod 2-1/2 inches wide from top to bottom and is designed to be used with a 3 or 3-1/2 inch pocket drapery, curtain, or valance.

Reader Tip

Since Continental® curtain rods were not designed solely to be used as valance rods, the use of an extension bracket is often required when doing so. *Continental® Valance rods are now available.*

The versatility of continental valances is limited only by one's imagination. Illustrations at the end of this section shows how using both size Continental® curtain rods and decorative rods in different combinations can achieve dramatic effects.

Another contender on the scene of phenomenal new looks is the rosette valance. It has a wonderfully elegant and romantic appeal, especially when done in sheer fabrics. Some are constructed with a pull cord that creates the rosette, while other versions are finished with the rosette completely intact. These valances are ideal for narrow windows, and may be multiplied on larger windows.

Measuring for a valance: Measure the area to be covered, including returns. Standard valance rods require from 6-1/4 to 8-1/4 inch returns. When using a valance over draperies or curtains, place the rod as close as is comfortable to the existing curtain rod without crushing the fabrics together. An inch or two should be sufficient. The length of a valance should be in balance with the length of the drapery or window treatment being used.

Reader Tip

For draperies, the valance should never be less than 12 inches long. The formula is, drapery length divided by seven. The valance may be longer, but never shorter than one seventh of the drapery length.

Priscillas with 20 inch long valances generally have 12 inch valances available as well, to be used with the shorter priscillas-63, 54, and 45 inch lengths.

Determining the width of a valance will depend on the type used. A pinch-pleated valance must fit the rod exactly, since the fullness has been pre-determined. The same is true of a pre-shirred valance, although not as rigidly. These kinds of valances may require tacking together with thread or straight pins as they will be available in specific widths as are pinch-pleated draperies. A valance that shirrs on a rod is easier to work with because of the flexibility of shirring more or less tightly. Simply determine the amount of valances to be shirred on the rod. When using a shirr-on valance over a shirr-on curtain, the widths are usually the same. If you have chosen to use three times the width for curtains, you would use three times the width for the valance. When using a shirr-on valance over pinch-pleated draperies it isn't as simple. Basically the two to four times width formula applies to any shirr-on treatment, but you might get some insight into accomplishing the look you want by asking a sales associate what size the window display is and what size or how many valances are being used on it. Use that information as your guide.

Continental valances may require much more than four times the width. Balloon valances and pole sleeve valances with three inch pockets, particularly the unlined chintz variety, display best when the valance is gathered as tightly as one can get it.

The pouf in balloon valances is created by stuffing with wrapping tissue.

Valances may be placed above curtains or draperies or in direct alignment outside of existing rods. Always consider the amount of clearance needed to clear existing rods and enable proper function of undertreatment. Some long valances may be placed at ceiling height, thus creating a ceiling to floor look without the expense of extra long draperies or curtains. Be sure the valance covers the pleated top of the draperies.

The use of valances over hard window treatments such as mini blinds or verticals has become very popular. Valances add a warmth; a softness, to what may otherwise be a rather stark window treatment. Valances also offer an opportunity to coordinate color schemes effectively.

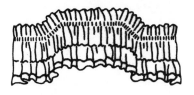

Fig. 47
This Arched Valance Is Achieved By Using the Mesa II Curtain Rod

Fig. 48
A Canopy Effect Can Be Achieved By Using a Close Clearance Rod On Top and Extending the Bottom Rod Farther Out

Using Wide Curtain Rods In Combination With Decorative Rods Can Create Interesting Top Treatments

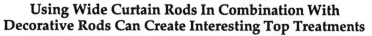

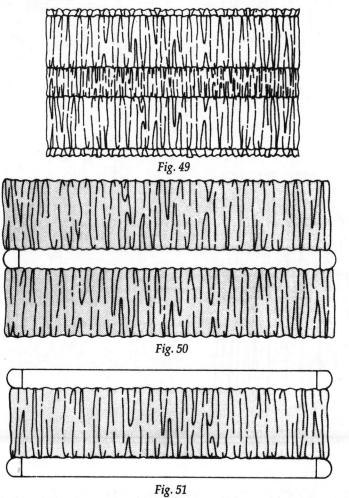

Fig. 49

Fig. 50

Fig. 51

Draping Sheer Fabric Panels Can Create
Unique Top Treatments

Fig. 52

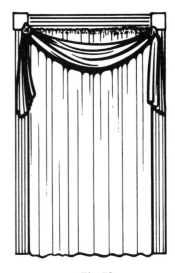

Fig. 53

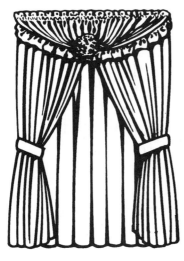

Fig. 54
Rosette Valances In Sheer Fabrics
Enhance Formal Settings

BALLOON SHADES

Balloon shades, or balloon curtains, are constructed like a rod-pocket panel, designed to shirr on a curtain rod, and often have ruffles at the bottom.

Balloon shades may be used as a primary window treatment or as an undertreatment. They are strung with medium weight cord through small plastic rings sewn at intervals across the width and length of the fabric. When this cord is pulled, it creates the poufs, or balloon effect that the name implies. To position the shade at any given length, the cord is wrapped around a cleat attached to the wall. Some shades have self-locking mechanisms and can be easily raised or lowered with the pull of a cord. Many balloon shades specify that they are adjustable and these do not imply that they are intended to be moved, once installed.

Balloon shades are available in specific widths and lengths. The wider the width, the more poufs there are. Two or more shades may be installed side by side. These shades are often sold with all necessary hardware including rod, but when the rod is not included, you would shirr-on a curtain rod the same as with any rod-pocket panel. Ready-made lengths are usually 48 or 63 inches.

When buying balloon shades, the manufacturer will list recommended coverage areas. For example, one balloon curtain is available in a 90 inch width and will fit windows 36 to 55 inches wide, and has four poufs. The larger size is a flat measurement of 138 inches wide and will fit a window width of 55 to 84 inches, and has six poufs.

These specifications will vary from one manufacturer to another, and also depends on the style of balloon shade. The widths and lengths available will vary, as well.

Fig. 55
Balloon Shade Under Panels
And Valance

41

Fig. 56
Balloon Shade As Primary Treatment
On Outside Mount

Fig. 57
Balloon Shade With Valance
As Primary Treatment—Inside Mount

MADE-TO-MEASURE
DRAPERIES

Made-to-measure draperies differ from custom only in that you will be doing your own measuring and installation. Made-to-measure is considerably more expensive than ready-mades, and equally less expensive than custom.

There is an area that may well be worth your consideration, strictly dollars and cents speaking. When considering top treatments alone—excluding draperies—you may find made-to-measure comparable in price, but only if you're considering an elaborate ready-made top treatment, usually using several rods and many multiples of valances. It would be worth your time to compare prices, bearing in mind that you will not be comparing prices on the same style valance. However, if you find a made-to-measure valance that you like equally as well as the ready-made valance you are comparing, and the price is the same, then you have another decorating option. The attractiveness of made- to-measure is the large selection of colors, prints, and fabrics.

There are circumstances where ready-made products will not achieve the look you want or fulfill your specific needs.

Reader Tip

The key to using ready-made products is in the placement of curtain rods to accommodate ready-made sizes.

When it is not desirable to move rods that have previously been installed for custom treatments, made-to-measure is another option.

Mobile homes are good candidates for made-to-measure. Many mobile home manufacturers install rods and draperies at the time of assembly. These are purchased in bulk and customized specifically for the windows intended. Because of the construction of some mobile homes, it is not desirable, or even possible in some cases, to anchor rods anywhere other than in a wall stud. Moving curtain rods could become a major undertaking.

Most made-to-measure draperies come pre-pinned and fan-folded. If your rods are already in place, it is simply a matter of hanging the draperies and breaking the header. For "breaking the header" see Pinch-Pleated Draperies.

When measuring for made-to-measure draperies, with rod already in place, you will measure the face of the rod from end to end. You will also need to measure the return, the part of the drapery that will wrap around to the wall. Returns are specified on made-to-measure draperies to insure that your first pleat is at the end of the curtain rod and not part of the return. The pair width you will be ordering will be the amount of the rod from end to end plus both returns plus four inches for overlap. To measure for length, measure from top of conventional rod to floor and subtract 1/2 inch for clearance. To measure for length on a decorator rod, measure from ring slide to floor and subtract 1/2 inch for clearance.

Made-to-measure draperies are often desirable because a fuller look is desired. However, this desire must be voiced to your sales associate. It sometimes requires moving into the next price range–as if for a wider width drapery. By doing this, you will have more widths of fabric per panel, to achieve pleats closer together. Without taking this into consideration, made-to-measure may not be pleated any closer together than ready-mades.

When ordering made-to-measure draperies for more than one window in the same room, when the windows are different widths, special ordering devices are required to achieve pleating of the same spacing on both windows. Be sure to discuss this with your sales associate.

Many made-to-measure drapery programs also make rod-pocket draperies, balloon shades, many different style top treatments, door panels, bedspreads, and cornice board valances. Fabric by the yard is also available.

Delivery time on made-to-measure varies from one manufacturer to another, but usually from one to two months is standard. There are sometimes reasons for delays that can not be foreseen, such as dye lot problems; temporary stock outages, or orders that have to be sent back for clarification.

Made-to-measure draperies are available through major drapery retailers. Although many retailers have discontinued stocking drapery departments, those who have continued are specializing in drapery products and are offering a large selection.

This is beneficial to the consumer as it is not as difficult to determine where to shop for window treatments, nor must one go from store to store to find an acceptable product.

Hard-to-Treat
Windows

$\mathbf{A}$ poorly placed or odd sized window may imbalance a room. It can be brought back into proportion with the correct window treatment. This involves creating an illusion, much the same way shoulder pads have in the fashion industry. Dressing a problem window is similar in that you will be building up, out, and around the window. You do this simply by extending curtain rods in the direction needed.

This works well for any type of window problem as long as the solution will coincide with ready-made sizes.

Patio panels and one-way-draw rods are very effective in the treatment of difficult windows. In fact, use of the correct type rod can be the complete solution in many cases. For example, there are rods made especially for bay windows of all kinds, corner windows, French doors, and more. **See Hardware.**

1. Corner Windows: A corner window is any window that comes together at the corner of a room. When using pinch-pleated draperies you have the option of using center-draw rods or one-way-draw rods. If each side of glass is large enough you may want to use center-draws, but keeping in mind that there is no room for stackback in the corner and each panel will be the same width when buying a pair. To keep the window balanced by having the split in the center of the window you can not allow for stackback on only one side.

A more popular treatment would be to use two, one-way-draw rods. You can still buy a pair—having two equal panels—but the stackback will be equal. You may have the panels draw to the corner or draw to the outside. You would not want the panels drawing to the corner if you're dealing with small windows.

This method of treating corner windows is ideal when working with glass of different widths. By using a pair of draperies, with two equal width panels, you are basically ignoring the fact that the glass is not of equal proportion and proceeding as if it were, and in doing so, are creating an illusion of balance. The end result is that you will be covering more wall space on one side than the other. When drawing the drapery open, you would only draw it to the end of the glass. Your rod can be adjusted for that purpose.

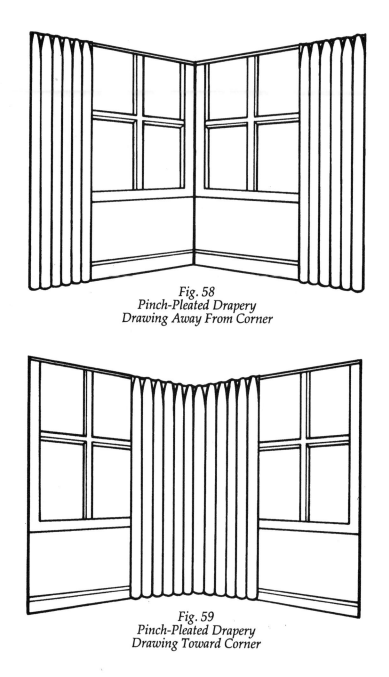

Fig. 58
Pinch-Pleated Drapery
Drawing Away From Corner

Fig. 59
Pinch-Pleated Drapery
Drawing Toward Corner

Priscillas are effective in treating corner windows, as well. Patio priscillas, because of their wider widths are a good choice. A pair may also be used on each window, tying the corner panels together as if it were one. One single pair may be used, placing each panel on the outsides away from the corner and installing a valance to cover the entire area.

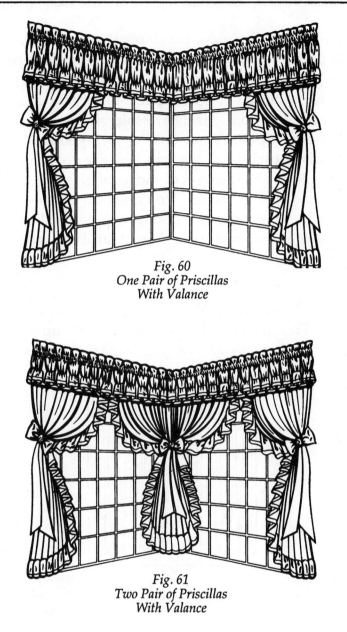

Fig. 60
One Pair of Priscillas
With Valance

Fig. 61
Two Pair of Priscillas
With Valance

2. French Doors: French doors may be either interior or exterior doors, and are characterized by their many small panes of glass which constitutes the larger portion of the door. French doors are always in pairs, and we generally think of them opening at the center. There are other types of French doors. Some have solid glass and some open only at one end. French doors may open outward or inward—one or the other, not both. The direction the doors open will need to be considered when deciding on a treatment. If the doors open outward there is no problem. However, if they open inward, you will need to allow for clearance. Rods will be placed, and drapery widths calculated so that when drawn, draperies will completely clear the doors.

If a lighter look is preferred, door panels may be used. A door panel is a flat piece of fabric with a rod-pocket at the top and the bottom, designed to be shirred onto a rod, and covers only the glass. Door panels are often brought together in the center with a matching fabric tie to create an hourglass effect. Sheer fabrics are most popular but other fabrics are available. Door panels are sold singly and always include a tie. Depending on the amount of privacy and the tying style you intend to use, you may use from one to four panels on each door. The standard size door panel is 60x72. 72 inches is the longest size available and it covers 69 inches of glass. The other three inches is taken up by the top and bottom header. You do not want the rod-pocket or header visible from the outside. When installing door panels, remember that you will need to place the rods far enough apart to keep the fabric taut. If the fabric is slack it will look untidy.

Pleated shades and mini blinds are frequently used as primary treatments on French doors. Hold-down brackets are used to prevent them from flopping or swinging when the door is in use.

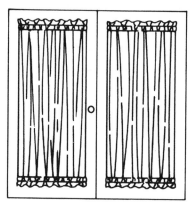

Fig. 62
Sheer Door Panels

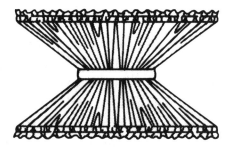

Fig. 63
One Or More
Panels Are Required to Create
Hourglass Effect

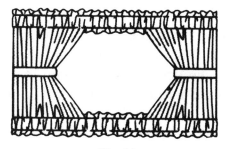

Fig. 64
Panels In Increments Of Two Are
Required to Achieve Diamond Effect

3. Bay Windows: There are many different types of bay windows. A circular bay is a curved window, sometimes called a bow window. A bay window may have three or more windows set at an angle to each other in a recessed area, sometimes with a window seat built in.

A bay window may be treated as one section with the proper curtain rod, the proper rod being either a single, double, or traverse rod, designed especially for bay windows. A pinch-pleated drapery would use the same formula as for any window, measuring the entire width of the bay and adding 20 inches. Bay windows may also be treated in sections, using a combination of center-draw and one-way-draw rods. When using stationary treatments with regular curtain rods, each window may be treated individually. Some of the new rosette valances don't show as well when combined on the same rod. Treating each section separately in this case would be to good advantage.

Priscillas are a popular treatment for bay windows, using multiple pairs in any number of combinations. This is an area where your imagination can really come into play. Experiment with pairs back-to-back and change the direction the ruffle faces. No other kind of window offers as many possibilities as a bay.

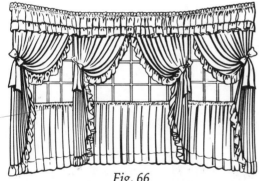

Fig. 66
Three-Way Bay With Two Pairs Of Priscillas,
Tiers And Valances

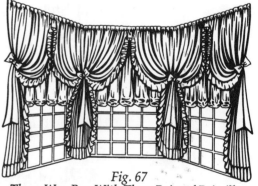

Fig. 67
Three-Way Bay With Three Pairs of Priscillas
(using four bows) With Balloon Shades

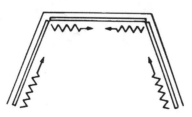

Fig. 65
For Pinch-Pleated Draperies, Use
Center-Draw Traverse Rod In Center
And One-Way Draw Rods On Sides

4. Double windows or multiple windows: Windows placed side by side, sometimes with a small amount of wall space between each one. Double or multiple windows are usually treated as one unit, ignoring the wall space as if it didn't exist. An attractive treatment for these windows is to use a pair on each window, butting the rods together, and bringing the interior panels together with a tieback. The wall will not be visible, and the effect, on a double window for example, will appear to be three seperate drapery panels. On a grouping of three windows you would use three pairs of draperies and have four sections of panels. A valance over the entire area will tie it together and create the illusion of one large window.

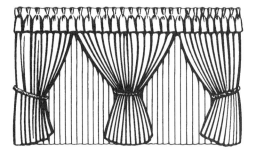

Fig. 68
Two Pairs of Draperies -Two Windows

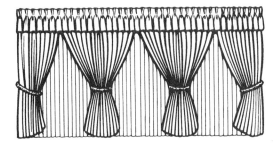

Fig. 69
Three Pairs Of Draperies -Three Windows

5. Palladian Window: An arched top center window often found in rooms with high ceilings. These windows, without the top arch, are otherwise easy to treat windows. The top arch is often ignored altogether and the bottom portion of the window is treated as if the arch didn't exist. However, ready-made treatments are beginning to become available, although still quite limited.

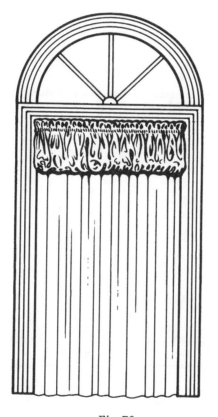

Fig. 70
The Arch On This Palladian Window Is Ignored And The Remainder
Of The Glass Is Treated With Sheer Panels And A Valance

6. Strip Windows: Wide windows set high off the floor. Floor length draperies are generally too overpowering. These windows usually require a 54 or 45 inch length drapery or curtain and a short valance. If a valance is used it may be placed far enough above the drapery so that it just covers the pleated heading. As with any short window treatment, it should hang at least five inches below the window so that the hem is not visible from the outside.

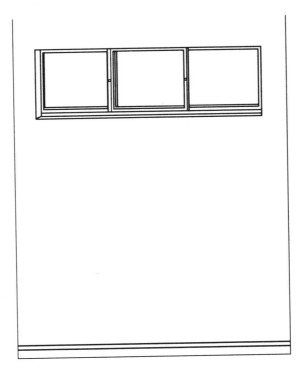

Fig. 71
Strip Windows Set High Off The Floor

HARD WINDOW COVERINGS

Hard window coverings include mini blinds, verticals, roller shades, woven woods, pleated shades, shutters, and wood blinds. Of all the hard window coverings, mini blinds are usually the least expensive. Whatever the expense of hard window treatments, it is comforting to know that it can be recouped over a period of time in energy saved; longer life of draperies; preservation of carpeting, and protection from furniture fading.

In climates of extreme temperatures, hard window treatments are an especially good investment. The more layers of window covering, the better the insulation. Many hard window treatments offer options especially designed for high sun exposure, such as thermal or solar backings. Vertical blinds are available with a hard plastic backing that protects the fabric and becomes room darkening at the same time.

Light, sun control, and privacy, are other benefits of hard window treatments.

Hard window coverings may be used as primary treatments or undertreatments. Many have matching valances. It has become popular to install a fabric valance over a hard window covering to soften the effect of what sometimes takes on a stark or clinical appearance.

Ready-made hard window coverings are limited in use because it is almost impossible to use one for an inside the window mount. This relegates ready-mades to outside mounts almost exclusively, and the fit is rarely ideal.

Made-to-measure hard window coverings insure an accurate fit and the cost is often not much more than ready-mades.

When measuring your window for an inside mount, width should be measured at the top, the middle, and the bottom. You will probably have a variance of 1/8 to 1/4 or as much as 1/2 inch. The measurement used will be the smallest of these three, to guarantee proper clearance. Measuring length works the same way, but the longest measurement will be used, to guarantee complete coverage. Manufacturers usually make their own allowances for clearance. Do not subtract or add to these measurements for any reason. When working with a sales associate at your chosen retailer, be sure to discuss the method of measuring and any concerns about measurements.

A Metal Tape Measure Should Always Be Used.

Plastic or cloth measuring tapes stretch and are not accurate enough for measurements where an eighth of an inch can make a difference.

Reader Tip

The width measurement is always stated first as with any ready-made or made-to-measure product. Costly mistakes can be made by reversing these measurements, as made-to-measure is not returnable.

Made-to-measure hard window treatments work the same as made-to-measure draperies, in that you must do your own installation. In most cases it is simply a matter of installing the brackets and then attaching the product. With a drill and an automatic screwdriver it takes only a matter of minutes. There are many businesses that specialize in installing window treatments. They are often companies that also clean draperies. The cost of made-to-measure plus the cost of installation from an independent installation company is still, in most cases, less expensive than custom.

HARDWARE

The key to using ready-made treatments is the correct use and placement of hardware to accommodate ready-made products and sizes.

Hardware is always the first consideration because it is the hardware that determines how your drapery or curtain will function. Do you want your drapery to pull to the left? You need a rod that will pull it to the left. Do you have a curved window? You can't buy a curved curtain, but you can buy a curved curtain rod that will curve any curtain for you.

There is a difference in the quality of curtain rods. Even Kirsch has a standard or heavy duty traverse rod. The heavy duty is by far the better rod. It comes with a cord tension pulley, whereas the standard one does not. The difference in cost is only a few dollars and well worth the additional expense. Another difference in standard curtain rods is the size of the nails or screws. The better rods will have larger and longer nails or screws. This may seem like a minor point—until you have to make a special trip to the store to buy longer nails. Strength is another factor, particularly evident with door panels where the panel is stretched taut between rods. You would be surprised how some curtain rods bend—difficult to maintain a straight line that way.

The following is a list of popular curtain rods and their function. It is by no means all that is available in todays market, but only a few of the most common. Rods described are made by Kirsch.

1. Conventional Traverse Rods:

a. Two-way-draw—
Designed to be used with a pair of pinch-pleated draperies opening in the center. Rods are available in widths from 30 inches minimum to a maximum of 300 inches. **Example of extendible sizes are:** 30 to 48, 48 to 86, 66 to 120, 86 to 150, 100 to 180, and 160 to 300 inches. Can be converted to one-way-draw. Cord may be on either side.

b. One-way-draw—
Designed to be used with pinch-pleated patio panels. Rods are available cord left; stack left, or cord right; stack right. The direction a panel stacks depends on the rod.

c. Double traverse—
Designed to be used with pinch-pleated draperies and pinch-pleated underdraperies. Center-draws, but may be converted to any variation of one-way-draws and cord positions.

2. Decorative Traverse Rods:

There are many different styles of decorator rods. They are measured from end ring to end ring and do not include the decorative end pieces, or finials, in this measurement. Draperies hang below the rod; rod and rings are visible. Decorative traverse rods need to be installed higher on the wall than conventional traverse rods. Measurement from the end of the hook slide to the floor should be 84 inches, to accommodate ready-made lengths. Decorative traverse rods always use a return. The brackets are mounted at the ends of the rods. Attach returns to the holes in the bottom of the bracket base.

a. Two-way-draw—
Designed to be used with a pair of pinch-pleated draperies. May be converted to one-way-draw.

b. Double traverse—
Designed to be used with a pinch-pleated overdrapery and a pinch-pleated under-drapery. Center-draws, but may be converted to any variation of one-way-draws and cord positions. A decorative double traverse rod has a decorator rod on the outside and an attached conventional rod on the side closer to the window.

3. *Cafe Rods:*

Decorative in design, most with finials, and available in diameters ranging from 3/8 to 1-3/8 inches; designed to be used with rod-pocket curtains or draperies with appropriate pocket depths. Cafe rods with finials do not have returns when using a shirr-on curtain.

Cafe rods with rings—

Designed to be used with pinch- pleated draperies and hand drawn. One side of drapery hook is inserted into drapery and the other side of hook is inserted into ring. One ring is required for each pleat and each leading edge. Returns are used by placing the last ring between the bracket and the finial and wrapping around to the wall to be hooked into the hole in the base of the bracket.

Wooden cafe rods use a different kind of bracket. To use returns, a cuphook or screweye may be affixed to the wall and the drapery return hooked into that.

4. *Utility Rod:*

A plain curtain rod without returns, usually comes with several kinds of brackets designed to be attached to conventional or decorative traverse rods for rod-pocket shirr-on undercurtains or used as an inside mount curtain rod with appropriate brackets.

5. *Spring-Tension Rod:*

A spring inside the rod holds it in place inside the window frame. It has rubber-tipped ends and is adjustable. Width is limited to a maximum of 72 inches and this rod is designed for light weight fabrics. When a wider width or stronger rod is required for an inside mount, a utility rod is designed for the same purpose with the exception that it requires a mounting bracket.

6. *Valance Rod:*

Designed for top treatments; may be used alone or over a conventional single or double traverse rod. May be attached to the traverse rod or to the wall. Projection is from 6-1/4 to 8-1/4 inches.

7. *Double rod:*

Two curtain rods with different clearances; using one bracket. Designed to be used with criss-cross priscillas, tiers and valance, or curtain and undersheer.

8. *Single Curtain Rod:*

Available in a variety of clearances. Layered window treatments require each outer treatment to clear the former one. Some clearances available are 1, 2, 3, and 4 inches.

9. *Sash Rod:*

Designed primarily for door panels with rod-pockets at the top and bottom. This rod nearly lays on the door, with a projection of only 3/16 inch. Two rods are needed for each door panel. Brackets at the bottom of the door are placed upside down.

10. *Curved Curtain Rod:*

Projects 2-1/2 inches at ends and usually a maximum of 8 inches at center.

11. *Continental®I:*

Designed to be used with pole-top shirr-on treatments with pocket depths a minimum of 5 inches. Depth of rod is 4-1/2 inches.

12. *Continental®II:*

Designed to be used with pole-top shirr-on treatments with pocket depths a minimum of 3 inches. Depth of rod is 2-1/2 inches. Maximum clearance is 5 inches from wall. When using for valances, an extension bracket is sometimes required. Continential® Valance and Corner rods are now available.

13. *Bay Window Rods:*

Since there are so many styles of bay windows, these rods are often not stocked by retailers, but are usually available on a special order basis. Bay window rods are available in single or double curtain rods, single or double traverse rods, and Continental® curtain rods. Bay windows may be treated with conventional rods by butting the rods together at each angle. Combinations of one-way and two-way rods can be used to create a wide assortment of functions.

14. *Wood Pole Sets:*

Styled like cafe rods, wood pole sets are popular in the treatment of bay windows and corner windows as well as other, easier to treat windows. With the use of special components such as wood pole sockets, swivel sockets, elbows, and double threaded screws, called connectors, treating any window in wood has become an easy task. Finials are used only on the outsides.

15. *Drapery Hooks:*

Use of the proper hooks in draperies is vitally important to achieve a correct finished look. The type hook required depends on whether the drapery has an open or closed header and whether the drapery will be hung on a conventional or decorative traverse rod.

a. Pin-on hooks—
For use with lined and closed-header draperies. Pin-on-hooks with a long shank are recommended for draperies using a standard conventional traverse rod. The long shank will hold the header upright. Used for master slides and returns as well.

Pin-on hooks with a short shank are used on lined draperies with closed-headers, when using a decorative traverse rod. Since the drapery hangs below the rod it is not necessary to help the header stand up. A long shank hook could not be used in any case because the hook is placed too close to the top of the drapery header. Although not the best choice in all cases, this hook can be used in any drapery, providing the placement is correct.

b. Slip-in hooks—
For use with open header draperies. There are two basic types of slip-in hooks; one is designed to be used with conventional traverse rods and the other is designed to be used with decorative traverse rods. The difference is, again, that draperies hang below a decorative traverse rod and hang slightly above a conventional traverse rod. These hooks, therefore, are not interchangeable.

Fig. 72
For Closed Header Draperies
Long Shank Helps SupportHeader
Use With Conventional
Traverse Rod

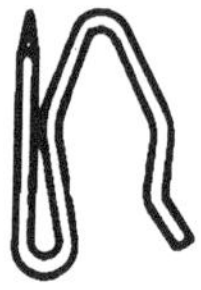

Fig. 73
For Closed Header Draperies
When Using A Decorative
Traverse Rod

Fig. 74
For Open Header Draperies
When Using A Conventional
Traverse Rod

Fig. 75
For Open Header Draperies
When Using A Decorative
Traverse Rod

SWAGHOLDERS

Use swagholders, 2-1/2" curtain rod or metal pole and two panels with 3" pocket headings.

Crisscross panels (3" pocket heading) on 2-1/2" curtain rod or pole; panels may need to be longer than usual. Trim by inserting contrasting 10" fabric square in center of pouf.

Gather square by corners, push in.

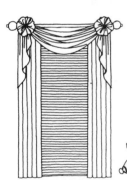

Use swagholders, metal pole and utility or curtain rod (for pocketed under-panels).

Use curtain rod for pocketed underpanels. Swags are formed from two panels and held by two swagholders at each end. Two pair of holders needed.

Use swagholders and rods as above Add two more fabric panels with 3" pocketed under-panels).

ASSEMBLY

Min. 2-1/2" clearance
Max. 5-1/2" clearance

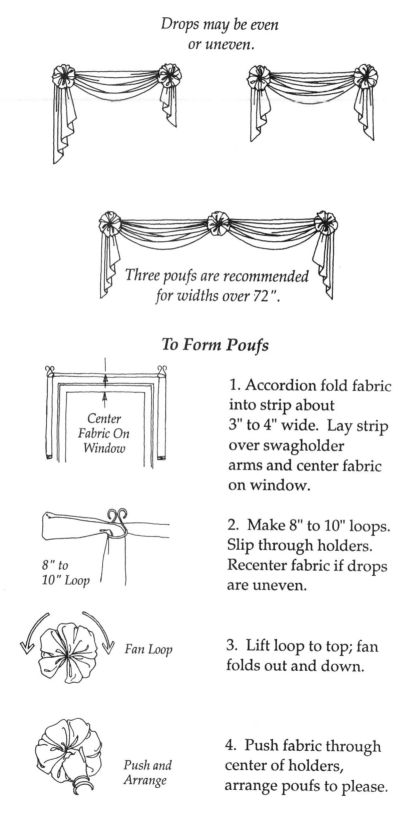

*Drops may be even
or uneven.*

*Three poufs are recommended
for widths over 72".*

To Form Poufs

*Center
Fabric On
Window*

1. Accordion fold fabric into strip about 3" to 4" wide. Lay strip over swagholder arms and center fabric on window.

*8" to
10" Loop*

2. Make 8" to 10" loops. Slip through holders. Recenter fabric if drops are uneven.

Fan Loop

3. Lift loop to top; fan folds out and down.

*Push and
Arrange*

4. Push fabric through center of holders, arrange poufs to please.

AFTERWORD

Congratulations! If you've read this book from cover to cover, you have become an expert. You can do anything you choose to do with your windows; effectively and expertly.

Decorating your own home can be a fulfilling and joyous experience. Watching it come together, step by step, is akin to growing a flower from seedling form. But, best of all, is the feeling of pride in creating your own version of Utopia.

Nothing says more about who we are than the things with which we surround ourselves. Home sweet home.